Grease is Just Grease, Right?

I0470913

Phillip Baker

ISBN: 1484047869
ISBN-13: 978-1484047866

DEDICATION

For my loving wife Jayne
I still don't know how you put up with me for all these years...

CONTENTS

ACKNOWLEDGMENTS

Some material is taken from Hydrotex® Lubrication University, Hydrotex Rookie School or the Hydrotex® Lube U webinar series. Our customers are welcome to attend Lubrication University and learn more about lubrication than you ever thought possible!

1 HOW I GOT HERE

How many of you have changed careers during your lifetime? I have - not once, but twice! I'm very lucky to have been quite successful in the first two, and I'm working very hard to be successful in the third!

My first experience in broadcasting was as an intern at WERC radio in Birmingham at age 17. I was working in the news department, and one of my responsibilities was to take the previous day's sound bites and transfer them to a reel-to-reel tape for archiving. I walked into the studio while one of the anchors was doing the afternoon broadcast and picked up all the carts - about 15 or so. As I was walking out, I tripped on the rug and all the carts crashed to the floor! The anchor, being a professional, never skipped a beat and went right on going. Yes, he yelled at me later, but I guess I deserved it! He went on to have a stellar career in broadcasting, too - his name is Steve Sanders, and today he's on WGN-TV in Chicago.

After a couple of years in radio, I moved to WVTM-TV Channel 13 in Birmingham where I worked my way up from teleprompter operator to assistant promotion director. Ken Snow, one of the news anchors there, got his pilot's license and talked about it all the time, so I got interested in flying also. My Dad was always an aviation buff, so I got that bug at an early age and it wasn't difficult to convince me to take flying lessons too. I got my license and really enjoyed flying around all over the southeast with my Dad. After I left channel 13, I spent a year in West Palm beach as promotion director at channel 34, but then moved back to Birmingham where I worked at several different places as a director and producer. After a couple of years of jumping from job to job, my Dad told me about an ad he saw in the paper for the air traffic controllers' test. I didn't know anything about being an air traffic controller, but I bought the book, studied a little, and took the test. I ended up making a 100, so I thought I might better check it out a little closer! Turns out they hired me immediately and I started my second career as an air traffic controller in Memphis at the ARTCC. The training program was intensely difficult and the hardest thing I have ever done, but I made it through. Less than 25% of those hired ever completely made it through the training program back then, so I am quite proud of that accomplishment. I spent 9 years in Memphis before I was lucky enough to get a transfer to Pensacola to the approach control. Now, you talk about difficult facilities! Pensacola has 3 very busy Naval air stations plus Eglin Air Force base just to the east, so the traffic is very heavy and very fast! Plus, most of the Navy flyers are trainees which makes it difficult to communicate with them (because they're paying more attention to flying the airplane) and they don't understand half of what you're telling them anyway. But Pensacola is a great place to live and Pace is a great place to raise kids (great school system!), so we've lived here ever since.

Early retirement is mandatory at age 56 with the FAA, and since I'm still a fairly young fella, I started looking around for something to do after FAA retirement. I ran across Hydrotex on Monster.com and was initially attracted to the description that it was "industrial sales," so I sent in my resume and a short letter to the CEO that I was interested. Mr. John Beasley answered me that same day and invited me to look at some documents they have that describe the company and the job. I reviewed the material and spoke at length with Mr. Beasley and a few months later (yes, I did some extensive research into the company and the industry as a whole), I agreed to become the Division Partner for the Mississippi, Alabama and Florida Gulf Coast territory. So in February 2013, my FAA retirement became effective and I started my third full-time career representing Hydrotex in the high-performance synthetic lubricant business!

I am extremely impressed with the way Hydrotex does business - they are not just a distributor, but they do an excellent job of consulting with the clients to make sure the lubricants they use are the right ones for each specific application. Also, when they build a lubricant, they don't just build it to the minimum specification, they build it to be the best possible lubricant for the application. What that gives Hydrotex customers is the highest possible reliability, the lowest long-term cost and the most profitability for your company.

It's called our Lubrication Management Process, and it's basically getting you away from just fixing things as they break (reactive maintenance) to a more predictive and proactive maintenance system, and saving you a ton of money in the process. Using tools like oil analysis, fuel testing, thermography, vibration analysis, and ultrasound can pinpoint problems before they become failures, and allow you to plan your maintenance to allow for minimum downtime for your equipment. Your highest costs aren't the replacement parts or the high-performance lubricants that you use, but if you lose a piece of equipment and your plant is not running while you're fixing it, then the cost of lost production is HUGE!

2 WHY LUBRICATE?

There are several different scientific reasons to lubricate: to reduce friction, reduce heat, minimize wear, seal out contaminants, prevent rust and corrosion and in the case of hydraulic and transmission fluids, to transmit power. But the scientific reasons are not why we lubricate. We lubricate for these realistic and sustainable reasons: to keep our equipment running, reduce maintenance and repair costs, reduce operating costs, reduce our carbon footprint, reduce energy usage and extend the life of our equipment.

Who's in charge of this mess?

The petroleum industry is really huge, and there are several organizations that help regulate and police the industry:

1. American Petroleum Institute (API) - This is the primary trade association representing America's Oil & Natural Gas industry. All the major oil companies are members - the big players, the guys that own the refineries - Exxon/Mobil, BP, Chevron, Shell etc.

2. American Society for Testing and Materials (ASTM) - This is the organization that writes the lab test procedures for the petroleum and all other industries. There are over 100 standard tests for the petroleum industry, and our labs in Dallas and Tulsa use about 20 of these on a regular basis. The purpose of standardized testing is so that all labs can get consistent results by using the same procedures.

3. Independent Lubrication Manufacturer's Association (ILMA) - Business association of oil related companies that don't own refineries. Hydrotex is a member of this association - it gives us a collective voice in the industry along with additive and base oil suppliers to address industry and legislative issues.

4. Smartway Transport - A voluntary partnership between various freight industry sectors and the EPA that establishes incentives for fuel efficiency improvements and greenhouse emissions reductions. One of the ways that Hydrotex has participated in this program is the development of a 5W30 heavy-duty engine oil formulation that gives diesel engines a 2% to 3% increase in fuel efficiency while still providing the same engine protection as a conventional 15W40.

5. International Standards Organization (ISO) - Establishes ISO viscosity grades and other quality standards, like manufacturing standards represented by designations such as 9001:2008 (which is what the Hydrotex manufacturing plant has). What that means is that we adhere to an extremely high level of quality and standard procedures while meeting the requirements of our customers.

6. American Gear Manufacturers Association (AGMA) - Establishes viscosity grades and other standards for gear oils.

7. National Lubricating Grease Institute (NLGI) - You've probably seen this one in regards to the grade of the grease that you use, and it's probably NLGI #2. They establish standards for grease. NLGI grades run from 000 (triple-aught) to 6, with #2 being the most common. 000 has the consistency of ketchup, #2 has the consistency of peanut butter, and #6 is like a cheddar cheese spread. The NLGI number has nothing to do with the quality of a grease - it's just a number that represents the thickness.

8. Society of Automotive Engineers (SAE) - This organization establishes SAE viscosity grades and other specifications for automotive parts and products. The current SAE standards for motor oil are CJ-4 for diesel and SN for gasoline. By the way, the "S" stands for spark, and the "C" stands for compression, which are the ways those engines provide combustions in the cylinders.

9. Society of Tribologists and Lubrication Engineers (STLE) - this organization promotes the advance of tribology (the science of interacting surfaces in relative motion - in other words, friction, lubrication and wear) and offers a process where individuals can become a Certified Lubrication Specialist that proves their knowledge and commitment to the industry.

As you can see, the industry is highly regulated and organized. Hydrotex is an active participant in the industry - we have many on our staff that have earned their CLS designation and are experts in tribology.

Friction

Friction is the resistance to movement due to the contact of surfaces moving relatively to each other.

Rub your hands together briskly. What happens? You feel heat building up, don't you? That's because your hands aren't smooth, so when you rub them together they create heat.

Even the metal balls in a bearing are not perfectly smooth. If you look at them microscopically, you will see that there are ridges and valleys on the polished surface - they're called asperities, and they will create heat when they rub across one another. If there is no lubrication, these asperities will touch resulting in welding and tearing of the surfaces creating friction and heat. This also produces large wear particles resulting in catastrophic surface failure.

How do we protect metal surfaces during startup before the oil starts flowing? That's called boundary lubrication, and it's a function of some of the additives in oil, like zinc, phosphorous and molybdenum disulfide. This additive coating prevents metal-to-metal contact by having less shear resistance than the metal surface asperities they're protecting. Hypoid gears are subject to notoriously high shock loads that tend to squeeze out lubricants, making the additives that provide boundary lubrication extremely important!

After the oil starts flowing, we look to establish a "perfect world" of lubrication - hydrodynamic lubrication. This is the where the asperities are separated by a liquid of proper viscosity and do not touch, thereby greatly reducing the coefficient of friction. It doesn't take much - a lubricating film of 2 to 15 microns (average of 7) will provide hydrodynamic lubrication for your engine.

Ball bearings have another lubrication regime known as elasto-hydrodynamic lubrication. This is strictly for rolling surfaces - it's where the surface of the bearing will deform (become flat) under load and then spring back to it's original shape when the load is reduced. The lubricant film actually becomes harder than the metal bearing surface therefore protecting it. This flexing also creates surface fatigue, which means that bearings will always have a limited lifespan due to this flexing, also known as hertzian fatigue.

3 VISCOSITY

Viscosity is the measurement of a fluid's resistance to flow at a defined temperature.

Take a look at the chart on the next page:

There are 8 columns on the chart representing the different ways we can measure viscosity - from left to right - Saybolt (SUS) viscosity at 100° Fahrenheit, Kinematic viscosity at 40° Centigrade, ISO viscosity, AGMA, SAE Engine, SAE Gear, Kinematic viscosity at 100° C, and then Saybolt viscosity at 210° F. You will notice that Kinematic viscosity at 40° C and ISO viscosity grades are very similar. Let's look at an example: a common hydraulic fluid viscosity is ISO 46. You'll see that the acceptable range for an ISO 46 hydraulic fluid, if you look to the left, is approximately 41 to 51 cinestokes (cSt) on the Kinematic scale, and approximately 210 to 260 Saybolt Universal Seconds (SUS) on the Saybolt viscosity scale. Now, if we continue to the right, you will see that an ISO 46 fluid is equivalent to an AGMA 1, an SAE 20 weight, an SAE 15W, and an SAE Gear weight of 75W. The "W" stands for winter weight, by the way. So you can see how the different grades of fluids relate to each other. What SAE Engine viscosity would an ISO 100 fluid be equivalent to? 30 weight! This is fun! Betcha didn't know that, did ya?

Oh, by the way, the most important physical property of a lubricant is

12920 Senlac Drive ♦ Suite 190
Farmers Branch, TX 75234
800.527.9439 ♦ www.hydrotexlube.com

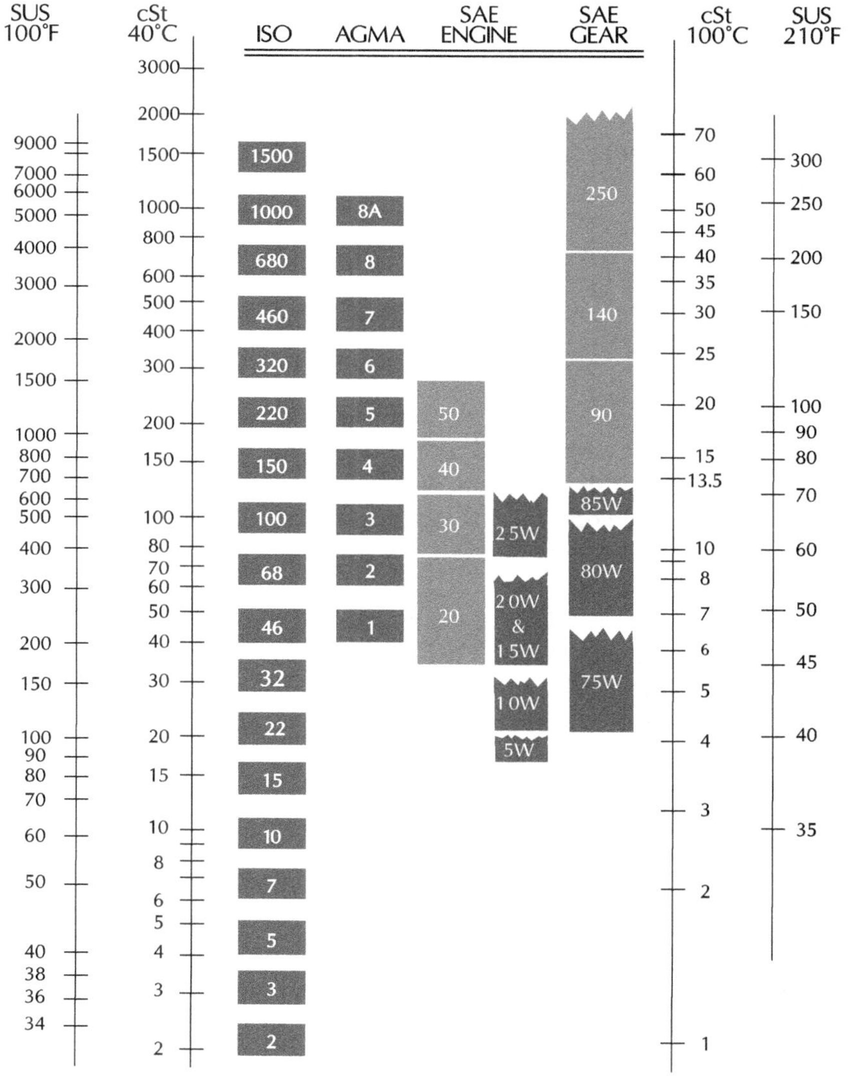

Your Lubrication Solution Partners®

SUS 100°F	cSt 40°C	ISO	AGMA	SAE ENGINE	SAE GEAR	cSt 100°C	SUS 210°F
	3000						
	2000					70	
9000	1500	1500			250	60	300
7000							
6000	1000	1000	8A			50	250
5000	800					45	
4000	600	680	8			40	200
3000	500					35	
		460	7		140	30	150
2000	400					25	
1500	300	320	6				
	200	220	5	50	90	20	100
1000							90
800	150	150	4	40		15	80
700						13.5	
600					85W		70
500	100	100	3	30			
400	80			2 5W		10	60
	70	68	2		80W	8	
300	60						
	50	46	1	20	2 0W & 1 5W	7	50
200	40					6	45
150	30	32			75W	5	
		22		1 0W			
100	20			5W		4	40
90							
80	15	15					
70						3	
60	10	10					35
	8						
50	6	7				2	
	5						
40	4	5					
38	3	3					
36							
34	2	2				1	

viscosity. If you don't have the right viscosity, you won't get the 2 to 15 micron lubricating film to achieve the hydrodynamic lubrication you need to keep the metal surfaces from touching!

I'll say that again: **the most important physical property of any lubricant - more than additives, more than TBN, more than anything else - is viscosity!**

Other important properties to consider:

Viscosity index: When first written, the VI scale was from 1 to 100. Now, the scale goes much higher due to the stability of some modern fluids.

Flash point: The lowest temperature at which a liquid can form an ignitable mixture in the air. The lower the flash point, the easier it is to ignite the material. The flash point of gasoline is -45° F. The flash point of diesel fuel is 144° F.

Pour point: The lowest temperature at which a fluid will flow when cooled under prescribed laboratory conditions. The pour point indicates how well an oil or distillate fuel will flow at cold operating temperatures. The lowest usable operating temperature of a fluid will be about 10 to 15 degrees above the pour point.

Oxidation resistance: The resistance to the chemical reaction of a lubricating fluid with oxygen present in air or with other contaminants. Every oil will eventually oxidize and need replacing. Synthetics have a lower rate of oxidation than conventional mineral oil. Note: for every 20° F increase in operating temperature, the oxidation rate doubles. In other words, for every 20° F increase in operating temperature, the life of the oil is cut in half. Conversely, for every 20° F drop in operating temperature, the life of the oil will double!

Emulsification: The ability of liquids to readily mix together and not separate. Most hydrocarbon-based products will blend together and stay together perfectly. Hydrocarbon products and water usually will not stay together - that's the principle behind lithographic printing.

Demulsification: The ability of liquids to separate after they are mixed. There are some instances where an emulsification is warranted, like with a soluble cutting fluid for machining, but when dealing with oils, you want them to be able to demulsify.

4 WHAT'S IN A BARREL OF OIL?

One barrel of crude oil contains 42 gallons. I have no idea why it's not 55 gallons, like every other barrel of stuff we deal with!

We can easily calculate price per gallon then of unrefined oil - last Friday's light crude oil price closed at $99.10, so if we divide that by 42, we get $2.36 a gallon. Last gasoline I bought this morning was $3.39 a gallon. With federal and state taxes (Florida) of 53.4 cents per gallon (American Petroleum Institute 4/2012), we get a gross profit per gallon of 49.6 cents a gallon (14.6%). When you think about all the players in the system - the refinery, the distributor and the retailer - all splitting the profit, and the amount of money that each would have to invest in infrastructure, then you can see that the amount each player makes per gallon just ain't that much. However, due to the total volume of product that flows through the system, then it makes it a very profitable business to be in!

The total volume of products that come out of a barrel of oil is 44.46 gallons, 2.46 gallons greater than the original 42 gallons of crude. This is called "processing gain," and it comes from the additional chemicals that are added during the refining process to create all the different products.

So what products come out of a barrel of oil? As you would expect, it's mostly fuel. Gasoline, diesel fuel and jet fuel make up about 80% of what's refined out of crude, with the rest being split between the petroleum gases (methane, ethane, propane and butane) and the products at the other end of the hydrocarbon spectrum, that being fuel oils, lubricants, asphalts and road oils, and coke. No, not the drinkable kind, but the kind of coke that can be used as a fuel or to manufacture graphite electrodes and anodes for the smelting industry.

Conventional base stocks contain some really nasty stuff - benzene rings, sulfur and other carcinogens. They also contain double bonds holding the atoms together, which are actually weaker than a single bond. Double bonds subject the molecule to shear, not only mechanically, but thermally and chemically as well. What all this means is that conventional oils break down and oxidize faster than a synthetic.

So where do synthetics come from? Synthetic lubricants are petroleum based - they just go through several additional processes after refining - hydrocracking and hydrotreating for most synthetics, and an extra process called hydro-isomerization that our fluids go through to make them into Hydrosynthetics®. Our Hydrosynthetic® fluids are pure branch chain hydrocarbon molecules that comprise the most stable, highest performance fluids in the industry.

Why is a branch chain molecule important? With most synthetics, all the molecules are straight chain, so the additives have no place to latch on to. Hydrosynthetic® fluids are 25% branch chain which means that the additives have places to hang. So not only do we generally use more additives per volume than anybody else, the additives we use will stay in place due to the branch chain molecules that our fluids have. Other synthetics have a tendency to "drop" their additives before the useful life of the fluid is complete.

5 ADDITIVES

The formulation of oils and greases is very complicated - many different components have to be satisfied and specifications have to be met. The basic formulation for an oil is base stock plus additives. The basic formulation for a grease is base stock plus additives plus thickener. Oh, by the way, we use grease in places where we are unable to use an oil - oils are the best way to lubricate, but sometimes we can't because the oil just wouldn't stay in place.

Many additives are used in oils and greases that perform different and unique functions. We will discuss the different additives for each kind of oil and grease starting with engine oil.

1. Engine oil additives

a. Detergents and dispersants (TBN) - used to remove sludge, carbon and other deposits and keep them suspended in the oil so they can be eliminated when the lubricant is drained. Typical compounds include succinimides, neutral metal sulfonates, metal phenates, polymeric detergents and amine compounds.[1]

b. Extreme pressure (EP) and anti-wear additives - these compounds form a protective film on metal engine parts to reduce wear and prevent scuffing and seizing. Zinc Dialkyldithiophosphates (ZDDP), tricresylphosphates, organic phosphates, chlorine and sulfur are

---

[1] "Engine Lubricant Additives What They Are and How They Function" by Dr. Thomas V. Liston, May 1992, Journal of the Society of Tribologists and Lubrication Engineers

common for these uses.

c. Oxidation inhibitors - prevent and control the oxidation of oil, the formation of varnish, sludge and corrosive compounds, and limits viscosity increases. ZDDP, aromatic amines, sulfurized products, and hindered phenols are used.

d. Rust and corrosion inhibitors - prevent the formation of rust on metal surfaces by providing surface film or neutralization of acids, using high base additives, sulfonates, phosphates, organic acids or esters, and amines.

e. Viscosity impovers (multi-grade products only) - reduce the rate of viscosity change with temperature, reduce fuel consumption, help maintain low oil consumption and allow easy cold starting. Additives such as polyisobutylene, methacrylate, acrylate polymers, and olefin copolymer are used. These may also incorporate dispersant groups to accomplish this task.

f. Anti-foam agents - reduce and prevent foam in crankcase using silicon polymers.

g. Pour point depressant - lowers the usable operating temperature of the oil allowing it to flow freely using low molecular weight methacrylate polymers.

And of course there may be other engine oil additives for specialized applications.

2. Automatic transmission fluid additives

a. Anti-wear

b. Corrosion inhibitors

c. Antioxidants

d. Detergents and dispersants

e. Viscosity modifiers

f. Anti-foam agents

And a few that weren't mentioned in the engine oil category:

g. Friction modifiers - used to reduce or modify friction characteristics of the metals and uses long chain polar compounds (amides, phosphates, phosphites, acids, etc.)

h. Metal deactivators - form surface films so that metal surfaces don't catalyze oil oxidation. Similar to oxidation inhibitors mentioned above - also uses ZDDP, metal phenates and organic nitrogen compounds.

i. Seal conditioners - optimize seal material in regards to volume (swell) and hardness so they are less likely to leak

3. Gear oil additives

a. Extreme pressure additives (EP)

b. Anti-wear agents

c. Anti-oxidants

d. Rust and corrosion inhibitors

e. Anti-foam agents

f. Viscosity index improvers

And two more not previously mentioned:

g. Tackiness agents - high molecular weight fluid polymer that resists throw off

h. Demulsifier - promotes oil and water separation in lubricants exposed to water

4. Grease additives

a. EP

b. Anti-wear

c. Rust and corrosion inhibitors

d. Friction reducers

e. Adhesive and cohesive agents

And a set of additives used more in grease than any other type of lubricant, because they would tend to settle out or be caught in a filter when used in an oil:

f. Solid lubricants - molybdenum disulphate, teflon and graphite - provides boundary lubrication in situations where a full fluid film isn't available or hasn't yet begun, such as engine startups.

6 GREASE

Grease is used in places where an oil won't stay in place, like in bearings and certain gears. Grease is also used on sliding surfaces and as a corrosion barrier film. The formulation of grease is the same as oil - base oil plus additives - plus one very important extra ingredient - a thickener. The oil in the grease is what provides the lubrication, but the thickener makes sure it stays in place.

You're probably familiar with the NLGI grade of a grease - that's the number that represents the thickness of the grease - and the scale is from 000 (triple-aught) to #6, with the most familiar being a #2. 000 has the consistency of ketchup, a #6 has the consistency of a cheddar cheese spread. Good 'ole #2 is like peanut butter.

There are many kinds of thickeners (soaps) that are used in greases, and they all have unique characteristics that make them suitable for different applications.

Grease Thickener Types

• Sodium

• Barium

• Calcium

• Calcium Complex

• Lithium

• Lithium Complex

• Aluminum Complex

• Polyurea

• Organic-Clay (Bentonite - will be described as Non-Melt)

• Silica

The most common thickener in today's high-performance greases is lithium and lithium complex - it provides extreme high temperature performance along with additional benefit of being totally non-corrosive. Calcium and aluminum complex soaps are used in grease designed for food grade applications.

Also, for the sake of argument, let's just say that all grease soaps are not compatible with one another (calcium and lithium soaps might be compatible under certain conditions). If you change to a grease that uses a different soap than you're using now, you should very carefully clean and flush your component of the old grease before adding the new grease. If you mix grease with different soaps, it is possible that they would thin and run out of the component, thicken and seize the component, or cause corrosion, none of which are good.

Characteristics of grease:

• Hardness - described by NLGI grade number

• Dropping point - temperature at which oil will separate from soap

• Pumpability - ease at which the grease will move through a distribution system

• Water resistance - oil and water don't mix, but water will, over time, wash away some of the grease from a component. Less is better, and the standard water washout rate test is ASTM D1264

• Acid resistance

• Oxidation resistance

• Amount of Tack - tackiness isn't always a desired property depending on application

• Color - based on what dyes are used. The color of a grease doesn't really mean anything, except that most grease with a moly additive are black, gray or another really dark color - because the solid moly additive is black.

NLGI grade is not an indicator of the true viscosity of the base oil the grease contains. Hydrotex manufactures several NLGI #2 greases, with base oil viscosities ranging from 24.1 (cinestokes at 40°C) to 5000.

A note about ASTM testing: Have you ever had anybody come into your shop and demonstrate the latest whiz-bang test that showed how good their grease is? This is fairly popular among some well known lubricant companies out there. But I have a few questions: Was it a standardized test by ASTM guidelines? Did they perform the test in controlled laboratory conditions? Testing done in other than tightly controlled laboratory conditions and not by ASTM written procedural standards should be taken with a grain of salt. Anybody who brings testing apparatus into your shop to prove the efficacy of their product should be politely escorted to the exit and thrown out on their ear.

There are a few general guidelines when using grease. First of all, make sure you aren't introducing dirt and other contaminants into your bearings by cleaning the zerk fitting with a shop towel before and after you grease. Grease fitting covers are a very inexpensive way to keep the zerk clean in between uses. Use a quality, calibrated grease gun so you know how much grease you are pumping into your component; this is very important in electric motors and other industrial applications. Also, do you keep your bearing packer sealed in between uses? If left sitting on a shelf, the packer will pick up dust and that dust will end up in your bearing.

Do you have electric motors or grease points in your system that are inaccessible? Then you might consider an auto lube system. Auto lubrication units can be installed on your electric motors to make sure the motor gets just the right amount of lubrication on a really consistent basis, and makes sure they don't get over-greased. If you over-grease an electric motor, you'll blow out the seal and the grease will end up on the windings causing it to fail.

Single Point Lubrication Applicators can also be used for inaccessible locations making sure those points actually get greased and increasing worker safety by cutting down the amount of times your worker has to access that location.

Single Point Lubrication Applicator systems are powered by either batteries that run an electric motor, or by a chemical reaction that pushes the grease into the component. They last anywhere from a couple of months to over a year depending on the volume of grease used. These units are becoming very popular for their convenience and low cost.

7 FUTURE OF RELIABILITY

There are four regimes of reliability in maintenance - reactive maintenance, preventive maintenance (PM), predictive maintenance and RCM, which stands for reliability-centered maintenance.

1. Reactive Maintenance

This is the old "run it 'til it breaks" maintenance. No planning or prevention, just operate the machine until something goes wrong and then fix it. You've heard the old saying: "If it ain't broke, don't fix it!" The government has a similar saying: "If it ain't broke, fix it until it is!"

2. Preventive Maintenance

You probably use this type of maintenance regime in your business or personal life. If you have a car that calls for an oil change every 3,000 miles, that's a type of preventive maintenance. Whether miles, hours, or by the calendar, any types of service done on a planned interval is preventive maintenance. This type of maintenance regime will save you 12% to 18% over reactive maintenance.

3. Predictive Maintenance

Did you know that 90% of all equipment failures can be predicted 6 to 12 months before failure? This is the premise of predictive maintenance, using methods such as oil analysis with wear particle testing, vibration analysis, ultrasound, and thermography. Predictive maintenance will save you an additional 8% to 12% over a preventive maintenance program by cutting down the risks of collateral damage and allowing you time to plan component replacement to decrease downtime. The obvious disadvantages are an increased investment in diagnostic maintenance equipment, training costs and management's resistance to change.

4. Reliability-Centered Maintenance (RCM)

This is the pinnacle of maintenance - the type of maintenance that can make your machinery run forever. Using a combination of the predictive tools from number 3 and adding comprehensive training programs, written SOP's, limited highly-select supplier partners, precision maintenance (balance, alignment, etc.) and lubrication excellence (cleanroom lube storage, delivery procedures and filtration), you can get to the most cost effective maintenance program available. By reducing the possibility of sudden equipment failures and focusing on critical components, you will increase reliability and save the most money in the long run. Again, the disadvantages are significant startup expenses, training and management resistance.

How do you get from a reactive state to RCM? It's not something you can do immediately. You should probably plan on a 2 to 5 year process of acquiring needed equipment, writing operating and maintenance procedures, training your maintenance staff and convincing all concerned of the benefits.

8 FUEL MANAGEMENT

After equipment acquisition costs, do you know what the largest expense is for a fleet operation? Diesel fuel. And nasty stuff it is, too. The quality of today's diesel fuel is generally terrible, and causes a host of problems in modern engines. The US Government has mandated that diesel fuel contain no more than 15 ppm of sulfur, otherwise known as ULSD. The process used to remove the sulfur also removed the lubricity of the fuel, so your fuel injectors and pumps don't get lubricated like they used to. Many fleets are now turning to diesel fuel improvers to get back the lost lubricity, as well as a host of other benefits that a quality fuel improver provides.

Let's look at the 7 Secrets of ULSD the Government Doesn't Want You To Know:

1. ULSD has almost zero lubricity.

2. It has more wax crystals to plug up fuel filters in cold weather.

3. It has less energy (BTUs) than before.

4. It has a higher capacity for water entrainment.

5. It has a lower amount of antioxidants that prevent corrosion.

6. It has poor thermal stability.

7. And the biggest, gut-wrenching property - higher cost!

Now, what are the benefits of using a high quality diesel fuel improver?

1. Cleans deposits from fuel injectors.

2. Improves cetane.

3. Restores lost power.

4. Provides added fuel lubricity.

5. Prevents fuel system corrosion.

6. Stabilizes fuel from oxidation.

7. Disperses moisture.

8. And the biggest benefit - pays for itself in added fuel economy. Proven by scientific laboratory and field tests - not just marketing hype.

A modern high-quality diesel fuel improver is a no-brainer to use - the only stumbling blocks I run into are bulk fuel tanks that have no access which makes it difficult to add the product. You usually need to have the cooperation of the fuel jobber so they can add the fuel improver when they deliver by dumping the improver into the fuel hose before they connect it up to the tank. There are also add-on dosing systems that will add the improver to the bulk tank or even while the vehicles are being fueled - these units cost around $3,000 each which may be prohibitive for smaller fleets.

When comparing diesel fuel improvers, there are a few things to look at to make sure you get the best value. Is the product EPA registered? Has the product been scientifically tested to prove the efficacy? Is it manufactured to ISO 9001-2008 quality standards? Take a look at the flash point (ASTM D56) - is it above 120° Fahrenheit? Then it might not have the amount of solvents to do the job correctly. What is the treat rate? (very important when comparing - look at cost per treated gallon of fuel, not the cost per gallon of improver).

Ask for and insist on a certificate of analysis from your fuel jobber for each delivery. They should provide it with no question, but they won't provide it unless you ask. Then, have your fuel tested independently at regular intervals so you know whether or not you are getting what you pay for. Have your bulk tanks tested for water and contamination once a year. Bacteria and fungi readily grow in a high water entrained diesel fuel, so have your tanks checked for those once a year also. Don't just use a biocide in a prophylactic manner - only use it when you need it because the bacteria in the tank can become resistant to the biocide just like bacteria in a human can become resistant to antibiotics.

A well-designed fuel management program will more than pay for itself not only in fuel economy, but in fewer failed injectors and less contaminated tanks.

ABOUT THE AUTHOR

Phil Baker is the Hydrotex Division Partner for the Mississippi, Alabama and Florida Panhandle Gulf Coast region.

Phone Numbers:

(850) 266-7788 (Office)
(850) 232-5389 (Cell)
(866) 355-5800 (Toll-Free)
(480) 393-4029 (Fax)

Worldwide Web:

www.hydrotex.info
phil@hydrotex.info
Facebook: Hydrotex Gulf Coast
Twitter: HydrotexBaker

Hydrotex Headquarters:

(800) 527-9439
www.hydrotexlube.com

www.ingramcontent.com/pod-product-compliance
Lightning Source LLC
Chambersburg PA
CBHW071555170526
45166CB00004B/1682